The Ultimate Screentime Playbook

Saleh Eric

Copyright © 2022 by Saleh Eric Ali

All rights reserved. No part of this book may be reproduced in any form or by any electronic or mechanical means, including information storage and retrieval systems, without permission in writing from the publisher.

The ideas and views in this book belong solely to the author and do not necessarily represent the views of any school, school district or organization.

ISBN: 9798795471235
Independently Published

Printed and bound in USA

For information about bulk orders, email salehericali@gmail.com

Illustration on page 43 by Erica Ryan

to my family
who patiently offer grace
as I figure out my life

Forward

Greg Fisher

In 2018, Saleh Eric and I started the Fathers' Program at the campus where we work. Initially we just thought it would be nice to get a couple of the dads together and maybe share some gems with them. We got the PTO to provide breakfast for us, because you know food always reels people in.

We had our first group and about a dozen dads showed up. We had some great conversations. The men really opened up about the personal challenges they were having raising their kids. Others chimed in offering solutions. We had Saleh come with the data and the professional education background. We had a pastor from a church show up one day and say a few words.

We had a couple of events where we brought the kids in and those days I will never forget for the rest of my life. We laid out a bunch of games like connect 4, dominoes and cards. We invited the kids to come in and play with their dads. I tell you, the excitement on the kids' and the dads' faces lit up the cafeteria.

The other time we brought the kids in was in Read Across America month. We paired the dads up with their children and had them read a story to their kid. I bet in twenty years if we go back and ask those kids about that day, they would remember the exact story their dad read to them.

If we could ever convene again, and hopefully soon, there's one thing I would like to say to the moms and dads. Some of you might think I'm joking when I say this, but I mean this with all seriousness. Your elementary school student does not need a phone at school.

I understand some try to justify it saying the kid needs a way to contact you. But believe me, if there's some type of emergency and you need to be contacted, there are professionals who know how to get you on the phone. The phone is simply a distraction.

We need to go back to the basics - how life was back in the day. You go to school to learn, and there's really no need for an entertainment device in your pocket. I just want parents to reconsider sending their kids to school with smartphones, especially in elementary school. I believe your child will be less distracted and it will be better for the entire learning community.

The Ultimate Screentime Playbook

Remember when your baby was three and he wanted to run in the street. You had to grab him by the arm and firmly let him know that playing in the street is dangerous! He cried and fell on the floor and when you tried to pick him up he arched his back and kicked his legs making it impossible to carry him (in a normal manner anyway). So you awkwardly held him however you could and he kicked and screamed but you didn't care.

At that time, it was clear to you that your number one job was to do what was best for your baby, even if he didn't fully understand what you were protecting him from. You knew that three year-olds are not privy to the dangers of the world. That's why they have parents. You knew that if your child somehow was hurt due to your negligence, you would live the rest of your life with guilt and regret.

I want to give you permission to go back to being that parent. The parent of a toddler. Whether your child is three or thirteen (or 23 if they are still living in your home) you maintain the duty to do your best to protect them from danger - the danger they realize and the danger they don't. Just as you refused to let your children play in the street or come near a steaming glass of tea, you still have the innate desire to protect the cubs from harm.

NFL games are usually played on Sundays. On Monday mornings, there are millions of heated conversations in offices around the country about what the losing quarterbacks should have done.

"He should have managed the clock better."

"He should have called a timeout."

"The idiot threw it right across the middle! He had a man open on the sideline."

"You can't take a sack in that situation! If anything, just throw it away!"

We call those people the *Monday morning quarterbacks*.

I want you to "*Monday morning*" your own leadership. You are the leader of your home. You are the quarterback. How would you critique your own play calls?

We are insightful when it comes to making decisions for others. We know all the correct plays in the last minute of a tied football game. But what about our own leadership decisions? How's that going?

Give yourself permission to embody that leadership role!

And take that job as seriously as you expect the president of the United States to take his. Why is it that world leaders have to make *all* the "right" decisions *all* the time, but you - the leader of your family - can be wishy-washy?

I'm putting *you* in the hot seat now. You are the quarterback, or the president, whichever moves you. And now you get the opportunity to practice all those Monday morning decision making skills.

The CDC (Centers for Disease Control and Prevention) estimates that children between the ages of eight and ten spend six hours per day on screens for entertainment. For teenagers it jumps to eight hours per day.

Research is slowly coming in on the effects of too much screentime - most of which is inconclusive due to the newness of the issue. But the information we have today is pointing to learning defects in children due to too much screentime.

Studies from the National Institutes of Health, another government health agency, find that "children who spent more than two hours a day on screen-time activities scored lower on language and thinking tests, and some children with more than seven hours a day of screen time experienced thinning of the brain's cortex, the area of the brain related to critical thinking and reasoning."

Void of statistics and research, if you are paying attention, you realize that your kids are a shell of themselves when engaged in their phones, tablets and television. The research may confirm it but you know your kids. If there's one thing a mom knows, it's her child. They're easily aggravated. They don't want to be bothered. There's little sense of humor and a lack of joy in anything outside of their screens. That's not who they really are.

If it makes you feel any better, you are not the only one dealing with this problem. It really has become a global pandemic and you are standing alongside tens of millions of parents looking for a solution.

It may also help to know that screentime addiction is not an accident.

Justin Rosenstein is an engineer who worked at both Google and Facebook.

"There are all these services on the internet that we think of as free," he said, in the Netflix documentary, *Social Dilemma*.

"They're not free. They're paid for by advertisers. Why do advertisers pay those companies? They pay in exchange for showing their ads to us. We are the product. Our attention is the product being sold to advertisers."

To think that your child's screentime addiction is simply a normal occurrence is to not understand what exactly is happening - to all of us, not just children. Imagine a job where you are paid hundreds of thousands (and in some cases millions) of dollars to make sure that kids' faces are buried in a screen as long as possible. That is exactly what's happening. And employees of these companies are starting to speak about it.

"At a lot of these technology companies, there are three main goals," Tristan Harris, another former tech employee, explained. "There's the engagement goal to drive up your usage and keep you scrolling, there's the growth goal to keep you coming back and inviting as many friends and getting them to invite more friends, and then there's the advertising goal to make sure that as all that's happening, you're making as much money as possible from advertising. Each of these goals are powered by algorithms whose job is to figure out what to show you to keep those numbers going up."

When adults, like myself, fall for this and wind up spending more time than they realize on social media, one may shrug their shoulders. But children rely on their caregivers to protect them from manipulation that leads to harm and addiction. If parents are not willing or able to be a shield, or at least a filter, then children are left to the mercy of big tech companies.

The sad irony of it all is parents, mostly unknowingly, are siding with these companies by subscribing to streaming services, purchasing devices and shoving them into their kids laps.

Game over! These kids don't stand a chance.

Let's fix this. Here's what follows:

- ☐ 28 Days to a Healthier Screentime Culture
- ☐ Grow a Healthy Screentime Culture From Birth

28 Days to a Healthier Screentime Culture

Week One

Today is the first of your 28 days to a healthier screentime culture in your home. This momentous day will not include any theatrics or celebrations, however, I'm going to ask that you do something you've probably never done before. Apologize to your children.

No, not one of those dismissive, half a second "my bad" apologies. This one is going to take a couple of minutes.

The purpose of this apology (and ask of forgiveness) is first to show your children that this process is not about *them* doing anything wrong. It's about *you* figuring out that you can do better and put them in a better position to be successful.

On this first day, children should feel no blame whatsoever. Instead they should simply understand that their parents love them and want the best for them.

Secondly, your apology is a model. In real time, your kids will see that even their parents acknowledge their own mistakes and begin a process of change.

Perhaps most importantly, the apology will symbolize that the whole family is in this together. This is not a grown ups versus kids thing. Lord knows you can't get off social media either. You want your kids to understand that this trail will not be hiked alone. You are all going to join hands and help each other to the finish line.

So what exactly are you apologizing for? For years you bought your child video games, smartphones and tablets and set them free. You set them free and you set yourself free! I know exactly what that feels like. There were little to no limits or guardrails surrounding their technology usage. And so for years, your child was left defenseless against the algorithms, behavior scientists and the brightest minds in technology at Electronic Arts, Facebook, Google and Tiktok!

That's not fair.

At dinner on day one, you will apologize for failing to realize this danger and protect your children from it. It might sound something like this:

Listen guys, I want to apologize to you for something. I try to do the best I can for you all and when I screw up, it really affects me. For the last five years, I've allowed you to use your phone and play video games with very little supervision. I was not aware at the time of how damaging that is for your studies, your brain and your mental health in general. It was totally my fault, I should have known better. I should have been more involved and paid closer attention to it, but I didn't. And my biggest regret is that now your screentime usage is an addictive habit that's going to be very hard to break. So I first want to apologize to you for failing you in that regard.

We cannot do anything about the past so we're not going to dwell on it. But what we can do is fix it starting from today. I'm going to need your help in coming up with a plan for how we - all of us - can reduce our daily screentime usage and learn to talk to each other, be creative and interact with the real world around us. I don't have all the answers. I'm not sure how we're going to do this, but I know we can do it if we put our minds together.

We don't have to come up with anything right this second, but I want you guys to think about it. We'll talk about this again tomorrow and come up with a plan.

For the rest of this particular day, do not talk about it. Allow time for processing. The kids will need it. I would hope that conversations of this level of emotion and magnitude aren't happening on a regular basis at dinner. So give them 24 hours to pout, cry, be afraid, think of solutions, talk amongst themselves, call a friend. Give space for however they process heavy information.

Because make no mistake, this is heavy duty stuff! For many of you reading this, you've never heard your parents apologize to you in such a personal, heart-felt manner. Have you?

And perhaps not so much out of arrogance but people often avoid the uncomfortable. And then for others, it's just culturally inappropriate to apologize to a subordinate.

You're going to set all that aside and make a decision to do things differently. The next month is not going to be easy. Change always leaves a mark. But no one changes just for the sake of change. There's always a prize at the end. For your family, the reward will be a more present household. One where you read together, go for walks, talk and laugh with one another. Your children will perform better in school, they will be less anxious and have higher self-esteem.

If this is worth changing for, read on.

One of the hardest things for a group of people to do is change culture. By nature we are copycats because we have a need, a true biological need, to be socially accepted. Our closest relatives in the animal kingdom are much like us.

Scientists placed five monkeys in a cage. In the middle of the cage was a ladder and at the top of the ladder rested a cluster of ripe bananas. As any normal monkey would do, one climbed to the top of the ladder to retrieve the bananas. When he got to the top, the experimenters doused *all* the animals with a blast of freezing water.

The monkey retreated and a second monkey tried again later. Again all five monkeys were punished with an ice cold shower. Eventually they stopped trying.

Then the experimenters removed one of the monkeys and replaced him with a new monkey who had never experienced the water hosing. New guy is looking around like *am I the only one seeing these bananas up here?*

He starts up the ladder only to be pummeled by the other four monkeys. They weren't having it!

He had no idea why he received the beating, but it was enough that he got the message; the bananas on the ladder are off limits!

Another of the original five was removed and replaced. Now only three monkeys in the cage had experienced the ice showers.

This brand new monkey, having never experienced an ice bath or a beating, goes for the bananas and is beaten by *all four* monkeys, including the monkey who never experienced the ice shower!

Again, the original monkeys were replaced, one by one until all five original monkeys were gone. None of the five monkeys in the cage had experienced the ice cold water showers. None of them knew why they shouldn't go up the ladder. Still, they beat any monkey who dared make an attempt up the ladder. It was the culture. Their natural disposition was to do what they saw others doing.

This experiment could very well be done replacing monkeys with people and the results would not be much different. Think about the things that we do that could go in the "that's how we've always done it" category.

Culture is hard to change.

It's day two and today is the day to devise a family plan. You will take input from the children but this is mainly so they feel they are a part of the process. People are more inclined to follow rules that they played a part in creating.

At the beginning of every year in my classrooms, I ask students to help us create a set of class norms that ensure we all stay safe, and grow the best learning environment for all. I already know what these rules are, but I want them to feel like these are their rules, not mine. I don't take every single recommendation, but if there is a recommendation that sounds similar to what I had in mind, I might say, "Oh that's a wonderful idea! What it sounds like you're saying is…" and I would go ahead and modify it to fit what I already had in mind.

There are two things your ultimate screentime plan must have.

One, you must have an agreed upon daily screentime limit. Second, there must be check-in dates, where the family comes together to check if they're meeting the target, and if the target is not being met, determine what adjustments should be made.

Keeping this in mind, on the second day, hold a meeting and ask for ideas on how the family can limit their screentime use in order to be more productive and spend more time together. Help the kids come to the conclusion that there needs to be a daily screentime limit. It's up to each individual family to determine this limit. I cannot specify a broad time limit. But use your judgment as leader of the home.

Fifteen minutes is probably too low of a limit and I think we can all agree that five hours is too much.

The goal is by now your children will understand how serious a situation this is and they'll offer reasonable recommendations. In the case you have that one smart kid who recommends 7 hours a day, you will simply say, "We're only going to consider reasonable ideas. If you can't be reasonable and take this seriously, I can figure it out myself."

You will also need to specify what qualifies as screentime.

Answering a phone call?
Scrolling Instagram?
Answering work emails?
Watching television?
Video games?
Online homework?

This specification is important because the lines can be blurred between work and pleasure. The Google Classroom tab is open, but next to it there's the Youtube tab.

We do it as grown ups. A million tabs open. And it's so easy to disengage from work and move over into entertainment.

Try this. Designate a location in the house for work and school related screentime. Work cannot be done anywhere else in the house. The goal is for everyone in the home to make a connection with that corner of the room and work.

If the kids see you at the work desk, then you must be doing work. When the kids are at the work desk, they're doing homework. You don't have to ask what they're doing. When homework is done, they leave the work desk and entertainment is done elsewhere in the home.

I worked from home for a year and a half during the covid pandemic and the kids were home with me. It was hard for them to make the transition in their heads that dad is home but dad is at work. They wanted to talk to me and ask for things and it was tempting because I was right there. Everything changed when I designated a workspace and told them, *when I'm sitting at that desk, don't talk to me.*

Designating a workspace makes it easy for you (and them) to tell the difference between work screentime and entertainment screentime.

Now, as a family you can decide if you want to combine the two in your screentime limits or if you want to only focus on entertainment screentime. Either way is fine. Some of you still work from home and some of you are back in person but regularly take work home. You may have high school kids who have assignments to complete at home and need technology.

In my situation, I don't take work home and the kids are still in elementary school and the need for technology is minimal. So these days we're only concerned with entertainment screentime.

Now, you've agreed on a daily screentime limit, and there are clear expectations. The next question is how to track screentime minutes.

There are a number of apps that track phone usage. *Social Fever* app may be a good place to start. It tracks your usage on social media and sends an alert when you've reached your limit. You can also try *My Addictiometer*. Neither of these companies are paying me to mention them. I wish they were.

The other option is good old fashioned scheduling. Schedule your phone and television usage. For example, if you set your daily limit at one hour, you can schedule 15 minutes of social media browsing at 7:30 before work, half an hour of YouTube during lunch break and another 15 minutes of television at 8:15 just before bedtime. At all other times you are only making and taking phone calls on your phone.

Finally, before day two ends, let the clan know that you all will meet again to check on the progress in another five days. Let them know each individual is responsible for his/her own self control and no one will be counting their minutes for them.

I'm going to now ask you to do something that will be extremely difficult. If you notice one of the kids is having a hard time keeping up their end of the bargain, DO NOT SAY ANYTHING. For these next five days I want you to focus mainly on you. The best thing you can do to help is be a model for your children.

They will screw up and go past their limits. Observe, but keep your mouth closed. Give them the space to work through this for a few days.

There will be an opportunity to check the progress and make adjustments at the beginning of the second week, which we will talk about now.

So let's recap what's been done so far.
1. You've apologized and taken the grunt of the blame for an out of control screentime culture at home.
2. The family came up with a maximum screentime limit that applies to all members of the family.
3. Five days have gone by trying the new guidelines and the first week is over.

Congratulations! You all really deserve to celebrate. Go out for boba. Believe me, many families will not make it even this far.

Week Two

When I was in school, sometime back in the Paleolothic era, teachers would teach and teach and teach. Then after a few weeks of working on a chapter, an exam was given and you learned if you passed or failed. This was also the standard procedure in the first few years of my teaching career.

Recently however, the pedagogy is changing in favor of more frequent checks for understanding and adjustments. The thinking is, the sooner you can figure out what students understand and what they don't, the sooner you can make adjustments in instruction. Why wait three weeks to assess when you can quickly check multiple times a week?

After five days of creating new habits and leaving old ones, it's time for a check. It takes eighteen days to break a habit. You will not see perfection after five days.

At today's family meeting, ask everyone to write on a piece of paper how well they think they stuck to the new screentime limit. Use a number scale of 1-10, with 10 being perfection and 1 being a complete disregard for the program.

Lay the self assessments out for everyone to see - this is a safe space. No shame. At this point, we are just checking to see where we are and how to get to where we want to go.

Then you're going to ask the simple question, "How do you feel?"

No leads, no prompts.

How do you feel?

Listen to the answers. And share how you feel. Often, people need to get the emotional part out before they can start thinking rationally. So give space at the beginning for the family to express frustration, excitement, accomplishment, pride, worry, etc.

Now let's get to the practical part and have a discussion. Here are some leading questions.

What's working?
What's not working?

Do you think the time limit we agreed to should be adjusted or is it fine?

What have you been doing instead of screentime?

What are some additional activities we can start? Let's share ideas.

One thing you will notice during that first week is most of the tech use is happening in private spaces and isolation facilitates excessive screentime use.

Raise your hand if your teen regularly disappears into their room for hours at a time, emerging only to eat and use the bathroom.

There's a fascinating podcast called *Rabbit Hole* that applies a magnifying glass on this fight for our attention. Caleb Cain bravely allowed New York Times columnist, Kevin Roose, to dig into his viewing history and his disheartening story.

Caleb was always shy and never really fit in at school. He got into video games as a teenager and everything changed for him. He got to meet online gamers, many of whom were in the same boat as he was - shy, lonely, aloof.

The gaming crowd is often looking for belonging. We all are. It's a need innate to being human.

The internet "was like an escape," Caleb recalls.

But the gaming world also introduced him to a plethora of characters and personalities that come with the world wide web.

Initially, those personalities were other video game players; strangers who come with all sorts of mannerisms, word choice and ideologies about the world. Strangers who would be more than happy to share their views with a young man who is craving purpose.

Then Caleb started watching YouTube.

He started out watching personalities who speak on politics, like Michael Moore. He didn't even realize he was headed down the rabbit hole as the YouTube algorithm suggested more and more videos in Caleb's interests. He binge watched atheist videos and began forming different opinions about God.

At one point he was hooked on Tony Robbins. He also went through an obsession with Zen philosophy.

By now, his routine was video games all day, and YouTube education at night. He was hooked. It was video after video and for hours at a time.

Eventually depression set in, as his focal interactions were between him and his devices.

"It's just me in a room and a bed," Caleb describes.

"If I wasn't at work, any single moment that I had, I was watching YouTube videos."

If Caleb's experience were an anomaly it would still be terribly sad. But what breaks one's heart even more is the unfortunate reality that this is becoming the norm for teens and young adults, not an exceptional outlier.

Never leave your children at the mercy of the alarmingly effective artificial intelligence of the tech world.

Loneliness is a killer.

Going into week two, set a hard rule: No electronics in the bedrooms and private spaces and we head to bed without electronic devices.

The power and influence of community is critical. We know the saying, *an idle mind is the devil's workshop*. Loneliness has a wide range of physical and mental effects such as drug and alcohol addiction, decreased memory, depression and suicide. Screens are an added element that intensifies those problems.

This is where you are probably going to get the most protest because there's comfort in being in bed, in pajamas and watching videos or double tapping photos. Sometimes people don't want to be bothered.

Regardless, you must set this hard rule - for the sake of your family and to protect your teens especially.

If your boys and girls are going to be on their phones or playing video games, it needs to be done in the living room or in a common space. There, the physical presence of the clan acts as protection from slipping into the lonely rabbit hole.

There are conversations to have with real people. There are communal interactions. People ask for help. The doorbell rings. Dogs bark outside. Mom wants to talk. Siblings want to talk.

Further, you can hold your teen accountable when you can see him. Yes, the *time* on screens is an issue, but you should also be worried about the *content* and your child's mental health.

And this is not about trust. This is us protecting each other. It really does take a village. Very few of us - even adults - are strong enough and conscious enough to understand how artificial intelligence is affecting our brains. Kevin Roose says in the *Rabbit Hole* podcast, "The internet is doing something to us that is profoundly changing who we are." And even if we do understand that, do we have the skills to avoid it? Alone?

That's an impossible ask of a teenager. Going into week two, the family will focus on two things:
1. Explore different activities to fill the time regained by less screentime
2. Practice using electronics only in common areas

During week two turn up the heat by using your voice as a reminder. Remember, in week one you said nothing. This week, be kind, and let your family know that you are watching more closely and they can count on you to remind them of the agreements. In week three, we will determine if cordial diplomacy is working or if we need to turn up the heat and impose sanctions.

Week 3

For many of you, you will hit your stride somewhere around the middle of week two and by the fourteenth day, you should be well on your way to replacing the old screentime habits with healthier ones.

With buy-in from the family and their participation in every step of this process, you will notice they are willing and capable of carrying their end of the bargain. During the second week you use your voice as a reminder and it will be well received, because you are all on the same team.

But these 28 days, of course, will not produce identical results for every family. Even within the same household the results will differ. We all have our own personalities and life experiences and we process things differently.

In the third week, you will focus on fixing the issues that words could not.

Which of the following kids is yours?

I'm going to say that I'm with the program but in practice I'm going to continue to do what I want, when I want until someone forces me to change.

I'm going to totally disregard the move toward a healthier screentime culture because there's nothing wrong with being online and this whole thing is dumb! I want you to know how dumb it is.

I want to adhere to our agreements but I'm having trouble with self-control. I've never been given this much responsibility.

    Your child who needs a little extra attention will likely be one of these. Don't be worried, and don't stress. You have a plan for that too.
    Numero uno, re-establish yourself as the commander in chief. You have the power. You have been sharing power, only because you *chose* to, not because you *had* to.

You pay the internet bill. You pay Disney+, the phone bill and you own the phones and tablets. Just as you giveth, you can taketh away.

Hold that card in your hand and this is a good time to display it proudly. In fact, punch a hole in that card and put it on a lanyard and wear it around your neck. Imagine walking around the house wearing a lanyard that reads, *I pay the bills and I own all electronics.*

The problem for many parents is they don't want to appear mean. When my six-year old accuses me of being mean, it stings. Even though I know I'm not, it still hurts to hear that.

It's hard to see your child hurting and even harder when that hurt is a result of something you did. I hear this from parents all the time. They refuse to use their executive power to toss the PlayStation in the trash (donate to Goodwill?) or cut off wifi on a teen's phone.

My kid will never forgive me if I did that!
That's a problem.

The fact that this device means SO much to this kid that he will *never* forgive you - that's a sign of how dangerously addicted they are.

If your nineteen-year old was living in your home, still receiving money from you and doing heroin, would you continue to fund his self-destruction?

Of course not. You would never enable and assist him in harming himself. You would stop giving him money. Even if, at the time, he thinks you're a monster. Because to continue to fund his misbehavior is to not love him well.

One may think this is such an extreme scenario that doesn't fit the topic of discussion in this book, but the common denominator is, you cannot be afraid to make decisions that will be painful in the short-term and prevent long-term harm.

Pain could be okay, if it prevents harm.

Let me say that again. Pain could be okay, if that pain prevents harm. Harm is a more permanent affair.

Pain is the burning sensation when you accidentally touch a hot stove. Harm is what happens when you keep your hand on that stove for sixty seconds. Pain just saved your butt from harm.

Starting on the 15th day of the program, you may need to change the wifi password, take back a cell phone or put the video game console in the trunk of your car.

But here's the caveat. When you restrict usage, it cannot be portrayed as a punishment. The message should be I'm doing this to *help* you, not to *punish* you. How do you convey that message?

Two things: first, you must explain your reasoning and second, speak with a calm, matter-of-fact demeanor. You are not yelling, you're not raising your voice, and be mindful of your facial expression. Do not give off a spirit of anger and frustration.

Hmm, I'm noticing it's really hard for you to regulate yourself with video games. Are you seeing that too?

I do trust that you can figure this out, you might need a little more time to figure it out, and that's okay, everyone is different.

But look, this is what we're going to do. Let's see if you can do a better job of regulating your use in the next 48 hours and stick to <u>your</u> plan and if it looks like it's still too difficult, I'm going to help you.

I'll help you by putting the game away and then we can come up with a schedule for when you're going to play. Another option is to just get rid of it altogether - that works too.

Remember, this conversation is happening in an almost sarcastically calm manner. This conveys to your child that you're not angry, you're not punishing and all you want to do is help. You will get better at this with practice. And the cool thing is, they will learn this style of conflict resolution from you. Everything does not need to be a fight and a shouting match. When they get older and have their own disagreements in their relationships, they will seek first to understand, then to be understood and it will bode well for them.

And then finally, stick to what you promised. If you made a verbal deal to take it away if certain criteria are not met, you must follow through. It will hurt both of you - if you have a heart anyway. But it's necessary.

My nine-year old son and I have a great relationship. We watch hoops together, we play chess and we talk often. A few nights ago we were hanging out an hour before his bedtime and his mom asked him to do something.

He threw a mini tantrum; some grunts, eye rolls, slumped shoulders, head thrown back. Right away, I knew his night should be done. I paused though, because we were having so much fun. We genuinely enjoy each other's company. Part of me wanted to excuse the behavior, but the rational side told me if this isn't nipped in the bud, we will end up with a disrespectful, self-centered teen and adult.

So I retired him for the night. He was distraught, because the infraction didn't seem like a big deal to him. I, too, was sad because now I had to spend the rest of the night with his mom (that's a joke).

We both felt that one.

When you use your executive powers, you will feel the pain. Understand that pain does not mean you're doing something wrong. It often means quite the opposite.

Short-term pain for long-term gain.

Week 4

How about holding this week's check-in at Starbucks or your favorite ice cream spot? Get out of the house. It's been a trying three weeks at home. Let's get a change of scenery and celebrate a little. Celebrate the good, the bad and the ugly.

Just as you offered all stakeholders an opportunity to share their feelings after weeks one and two, begin week four by asking the troops how they feel. What's been the best part of the last three weeks, what's been the most challenging? And if your kids have any sense of humor, there will for sure be some snarky comments. A little humor may be welcome at this point. A lot of emotional energy has been expended getting the plane off the ground. The hope is by now you are entering cruise mode.

Think of the previous twenty-one days as the take-off and climb of an aircraft. A ton of energy, fuel and pilot attention is required to lift a 20-ton piece of metal into the air and then climb to an elevation of 35,000 feet.

Once the plane has hit cruise altitude the pilot can release some control and shut off the seatbelt light. Much less energy is used for the duration of the flight, including the landing. Aviation people like to say landing is just a controlled crash.

The next seven days should be less taxing on all and require less intensity. However, no two situations are identical and one size definitely does not fit all. For some, it may take a bit more time to enter cruise mode.

In the event that you had to restrict accessibility to electronics in week three, consider releasing some control for week four.

Have this conversation with your family.

I would simply ask the question.

So, I'm thinking about releasing some control back to you. I think you can handle it, what about you? Do you think you're getting better with self-regulation?

Your vote of confidence in your child means the world to them! Even if you don't actually trust they're ready, always show them that you believe in their abilities. Kids will act on what they truly *believe* their parents think of them. Speak it into existence.

And if you all determine that "sanctions" should continue a bit further, that's fine too. You may start to get tired and frustrated in this case. Be proactive in expecting some discouragement and frustration. Breathe. Take long, slow, deep breaths. You're *right* there! But the job is not finished.

If you were fortunate enough not to have restricted use during week three, then more than likely you are in cruise mode for week four. Congratulations! The "finish" line is just days ahead. And of course, I'm using air quotes because this work is never completely done.

Looking ahead to the final days of your 28 days (and beyond) to a healthier screentime culture, you might have to take more of an active role in helping your children find things to do. Because this is a real challenge for children born after 2010.

On my bookshelf in my living room, there is a Lego model of the Dubai skyline that I built myself. I used the instructions, but still. Legos are a childhood pastime for me. Today, I still enjoy breaking open those clear plastic bags and dumping the pieces out onto the carpet as I begin a new structure.

The act of building is gratifying but more importantly, especially for young developing brains, it's an activity that requires an active brain as opposed to a passive one.

You can classify most activities into either an active brain activity or a passive brain activity. Active brain hobbies often produce a product or require deep critical thinking. Passive brain activities produce nothing. Children simply absorb or consume a product - a product that was created by an active brain, by the way.

Think of a child watching television - Paw Patrol, a Disney movie or a YouTube creator. The child's brain is passive as information is being fed into the brain. Meanwhile it takes very little effort to disseminate that information as the primary purpose is entertainment.

Now imagine that same child with a set of building instructions and seven hundred building pieces before him. In this activity, the child must *actively* read the instructions, make sense of the models and then with his hands, build a representation of what he has read and seen into a real life structure. This is an active brain.

This is a brain that, given regular opportunities to work at a high capacity, will do better at solving multi-step math word problems, making inferences and predictions when reading a text and writing clear and coherent pieces.

It's unfair to ask an eleven year old to produce active brain products in school when their brains have very little experience in active brain activities at home.

The brain is in fact like a muscle. The more it's used, the stronger and more effective it becomes. The less it's used, the less effective it is. If you've ever broken a bone and had to wear a cast for four to six weeks, do you remember what that limb felt like when the cast was finally removed? Remember how difficult and painful it was to move the injured limb? You lacked a full range of motion. Perhaps you lost some muscle mass.

Similarly, a passive brain finds difficulty being productive when called upon. Even the elderly are advised to continue working or volunteering in some capacity in retirement to offset deterioration of the brain. It is not uncommon to see folks in retirement homes playing cards, board games and solving crossword puzzles.

This brings us to one of my most highly recommended activities...reading. Is it an active or a passive interest?

Reading appears to toe the line between active and passive. As with watching television, information is being received instead of produced. However, unlike watching television or YouTube videos, reading requires the active task of making out the words on the pages and there's also a heightened level of critical and deep thinking involved.

Even for adults who are solid readers, reading a book still requires focus. The setting must be right - a quiet room, maybe the mood of a comfortable coffee shop. For children who are early readers, the act of reading requires even more focus because the challenge is greater. The same cannot be said for watching TV. Neither challenge, nor focus are required.

In terms of critical thinking skills, there is a difference in fictional reading, which is mainly reading for pleasure, and nonfiction, which can be and often is a joyful experience and dives into real-life concepts. To fully comprehend (and enjoy) an informational text, readers are required to activate prior knowledge, make connections to real life situations, make connections to *other* texts and very importantly they are required to think!

Reading nonfiction texts could be classified as a *more* active activity than reading fiction, and a balance of both is not a bad idea.

active	passive
➢ reading ➢ building ➢ pretend play ➢ chess ➢ playing sports ➢ creating music ➢ writing ➢ cooking ➢ creating art	➢ watching TV ➢ watching YouTube creators ➢ listening to music ➢ exploring social media ➢ watching sports

The best position to be in, of course, is for this screentime revamping to not even be necessary in your home. If you never take a sip of alcohol, you will never have to go to Alcoholics Anonymous, right?

But how do you manage the use of something that's unavoidable? Smartphones are as much a part of our world as cars. They cannot be totally avoided. There must be a way to integrate television, apps and smartphones without it spiraling out of control.

The next section focuses on starting from birth. How can we raise our kids through the years with screentime habits that do not turn into addiction?

Grow a Healthy Screentime Culture From Birth

How Did We Get Here?

In a small way, I was part of the beginning of the smartphone evolution. In the early years of the new millennium, Sprint (now defunct) was looking for salespeople for their new, revolutionary phones. The ideal employee would not so much be selling the phones as they would be teaching people how to use them in all their futuristic features.

I got the job and they gave the sales team tutorials on these phones. Some were small, curved flip phones with cameras on the front! Others were the basic rectangular-shaped, also with cameras. As you can imagine, these were very blurry, pixelated photos, but no one knew that at the time. The phone had a camera! End of story.

You could log on to the web by opening the browser and typing in the web address. It took thirty to forty-five seconds, but the grainy website would eventually pop up and you could scroll with the arrow button and see a miniature version of the actual webpage! I mean this stuff was mind blowing.

Sprint gave us phones for our own personal use. They said, if we're going to show people the functionality of the devices, we need to be using them personally. How bad would it look to be selling Sprint while holding a Verizon (our biggest competitor at the time) phone in my back pocket?

I had the PM8920. That joker was slick. Google it. I bet there's one of those in a museum somewhere. It had a 1.3 megapixel camera and went for about $150, without accessories. We were taught to push accessories - car chargers, headphones - that's where the big profit margins were.

They placed me inside Radio Shack and I stood in front of the locked phone cases with access to open the container and show the phones to potential customers.

The great thing about this one is you can take a picture anytime you want. All you have to do is flip it open and press this button. Check this out…*click*…see, that's you!

Look, you can also send messages to your friends - if they have a Sprint phone. This button is for a, b and c, if you press it once it will give you a, twice gives you b and three times is c. It's really easy.

Apple was still not in the phone business in 2004. They were making ipods and improving upon the Mac desktop computers that put them on the map. Apple released its first smartphone in 2008 - a sleek design with an amazing 2 megapixel camera and, wait for it...touch screen!

As smartphone technology exponentially improved year over year, the video gaming industry was not to be left behind. In 2008, the top four selling video games worldwide were all Wii games: *Wii Sports*, *Mario Kart Wii*, *Wii Fit* and *Wii Play*. Wii is known for being somewhat active as gamers must move their bodies physically to play the game. These were also games that, for the most part, were played at home interactively with family.

The following year, *Call of Duty: Modern Warfare 2* crept into the top three sales list. By 2011, another installment of the Call of Duty series,

Black Ops 2, was the top grossing video game at a whopping $1 billion in sales.

By 2019 as the graphics and interactivity soared to new heights, *Fortnite* became the top grossing video game at $3.7 billion in sales! Gone were the days when video games were simply played at home with family or neighbors. When I was a teen we knew the only two kids in the neighborhood who had a video game console. If you wanted to play, you went to either of their homes, played for an hour or so and then went back outside.

Today, with the improvement in video game technology and the advent of online gaming, kids can strap on a headset and play interactively with multiple friends, each from the comfort of their own homes. The scary thing is kids can play interactively with total strangers. The two (sometimes more) gamers are able to speak to each other in real time as they strategize their way through the levels.

There's a 35-year old man in his mother's basement in Topeka, Kansas playing video games with your twelve-year old son. Manchild is in boxers, wearing a headset, speaking to your kid about the game…and whatever else he wishes.

The decade between 2010 and 2020 also brought on the mother of all babysitters.

The iPad!

The $1,000 Babysitter

The personal tablet was simply a brilliant invention. Yes, it can be used to check email, draw, edit video and watch television shows. But the true brilliance of the iPad is its ability to babysit.

Toddler is crying? Plop an iPad before her and run Cocomelon.

Need to get some cooking done?

Dining at a restaurant with the kids?

Going on a road trip?

Complaints about boredom?

Just need some alone time? Tired of answering questions?

Have a thirty minute wait at the doctor's office or the DMV?

The tablet is your babysitting solution. It's the $1,000 babysitter. Before 2010, parents used to hire human babysitters or an older sibling would do the job. But that's no longer necessary.

The crazy thing is, the culture has deviated to the point that a tablet in the hands of a 3-year-old is somewhat of a status symbol for young parents.

Look what I can do for my child. She has her own tablet. I'm doing well for her.

In literally one generation we went from flip phones used mainly for calling and occasional texting to hours upon hours of video gaming, tablets as babysitters and parents with faces buried in their phones.

Make a Decision

When your child is born, you and your spouse need to make a conscious decision on whether or not screens will be routine in your home. You should explicitly have this conversation. The problem is many people don't even think about it. It's not even a discussion that comes up. This is a personal decision parents should make and there's no right or wrong answer. But I can tell you what we did; it has worked for us.

We decided early on that the normal disposition in our home is with the television off. We do have one but it's not running all day. Our kids are not at liberty to turn on and watch at their leisure and adults are not watching regularly either.

When we are watching TV it's a family movie night, there's a sporting event or maybe mom and I are watching *House Hunters* when the kids are down. But we intentionally decided against having the television running as a normal routine of life.

We do have an iPad. But it's one iPad for the family, not one for each member of the family. The tablet has a password on it and our two children (both under 10) need permission to use it. The tablet is almost an afterthought because they know what the answer is nine times out of ten. Unless they're at grandma's, that's another story.

They'll usually use the iPad on a Friday night or we might randomly let them use it. Truth be told, the reason we bought it in the first place was for long plane rides.

We were standing in Best Buy and the original thought was to buy two so they could have their own tablet on the plane. But we decided to get only one and force them to communicate with each other and agree on what to watch. They would be forced to enjoy whatever they were doing together instead of entertaining themselves separately.

And no, I was not just being cheap. It wasn't about the money. The trip we were prepping for was 10x what those two tablets would have cost. Just because you can afford something doesn't make it a good idea.

Screentime is not a predictable option for our kids so they find other things to do - similar to how you probably grew up, if you're as old as I am. So the question remains, what can kids do to stay busy and entertained without screens in a culture of screens?

I'm Bored!

Next time the kids complain about boredom, tell them, "Oh that's nice. It's good to be bored sometimes."

Boredom is not an alarm you need to immediately silence. But that goes against our natural parental tendency to rush to our kids' rescue anytime they experience any type of discomfort. Complaints from our children tug on our emotional heartstrings. We feel we're doing something wrong or failing them if they're bored. Stop that.

Life is not always exciting. They need to understand this. They're not going to always be deeply engaged and entertained. And that's okay. Boredom is part of life. There is no need to rush and put that fire out. In fact, when you do, it's going to become increasingly difficult to cure their boredom as the dopamine receptors in the brain will require more and more stimulus in order to fire up and satisfy your children.

In her 2021 book *Dopamine Nation*, Anna Lembke, MD, goes into depth about the human tendency to obsessively chase pleasure and avoid discomfort. On boredom she writes:

Boredom is not just boring. It can also be terrifying. It forces us to come face-to-face with bigger questions of meaning and purpose. But boredom is also an opportunity for discovery and invention. It creates the space necessary for a new thought to form, without which we're endlessly reacting to stimuli around us, rather than allowing ourselves to be within our lived experience.

Long and consistent bouts of boredom, however, is a recipe for harm. We don't want our kids to be chronically bored. That's a torturous existence for a human being. Afterall, boredom is one of the pains of incarceration.

So how do we keep kids busy (and out of the way) without screens?

The most important thing - and probably most difficult for parents to accept - is you have to be a model. Your children are going to do what they see you doing.

I've been guilty of this. If you follow me on Instagram, you know I often have binge days. I have a relationship with my son where he can, and has, called me out on my screentime usage.

If you want your kids to read, you have to read. If you want them to play board games, you have to play them. If you want them to work, you have to work. If you want them to clean the house, you have to clean the house. If you want them outside, you have to spend time outdoors.

And there will be valid excuses - the chief among them being, I'm tired and I work too much.

I will never diminish a family's personal struggles. Every situation is different and family dynamics differ drastically. I have had students whose parents leave for work when the kids get home from school and get back just as the kids are getting up for school in the morning.

Many men and women are raising their children alone. I do not fully understand that challenge.

Whatever your situation, figure out how you could be a model for your children. When you're at home with them, limit your screentime usage and watch them follow your lead.

In addition to modeling, I want you to provide substitutes for screens. Just as you paid for their gaming console and cell phones, you can fund substitutes.

Again, every family is different and people's interests are different, but I'll share some substitutes that have worked in my home.

We take regular trips to the library. It's free and the kids LOVE it. But this is because it's always been a part of our family culture. Keep in mind, if your kids were already addicted to screens and you were going through the 28-day program, it's going to be difficult to all of a sudden do library trips.

That's boring!

Yeah of course it is, because the library cannot compete with Epic Games. Remember, this section focuses on starting from scratch; avoiding the fire, not extinguishing it.

Occasionally we'll get new Lego sets. The kids spend a couple days building them, a few more playing with them and then they move on from it until they get a new set. I still enjoy the building process as an adult.

Puzzles are another brain stimulating, time consuming activity. My kids never caught on to puzzles but my 5-year-old nephew never met a puzzle he didn't want to complete. Believe it or not he's conquered a 500-piece puzzle.

Break up the monotony with just twenty minutes outdoors together. Go for a brisk walk. Sit outside and read. Kick a soccer ball around. And sometimes we just kick the kids out.

I'm bored.
Go outside.
I don't want to go outside.

No, go outside! And don't come back for 20 minutes.

Then close the door behind them and lock it.

Your kids can also help with the chores. Even if they can't do it alone, they can work side by side with you. They can fold and put away laundry, put away dishes, set the dinner table, clean their room, dust furniture, etc.

The most surprising thing, however, is that without screens, your kids will find interest in things that you would never have imagined. Don't underestimate the creativity of children. Just think about it. What did you do as a kid?

My kids do some really weird things. The other day, they had all twenty-five of their stuffed animals in a line. They had a piece of paper and they listed the names of each animal and what made-up powers they have.

Without screens, children will regularly pretend play. Pretend play is an active brain activity. Children create the characters, conflict and resolution instead of Disney doing that for them.

You cannot really predict what interests they will find. But they will develop some interests. It may be art, journaling, crafts, animals, music, or drama. Don't let screens stifle their curiosity and creativity.

The Case Against Video Games

With anything that carries benefit but also some downside or risk, the best way to look at it is to weigh the pros vs the cons and then determine if the benefit is worth the potential negative that may occur. That's what we will do here.

The obvious draw for video games is entertainment. It's fun. I grew up playing Madden and NBA Live. I recently returned from a stay at a holiday home in the mountains. In the basement was an old Pacman game, complete with the joystick and all. I couldn't pull myself away from that table. It was so much fun!

That's pretty much where the benefit ends. I would compare it to a trip to Disneyland, Six Flags or a sporting event. You go because it's fun. That's it.

Unfortunately, video games are highly addictive. When gamers get hooked, they're hooked! Many of you have seen it in your own kids. You ask them to turn off the game and the tantrum that ensues is not unlike a heroin addict after being refused a needle. I don't want anything to have that level of control in my home.

I've seen this addiction follow boys into adulthood. They cannot let go of the games long enough to study and focus on their long term life goals. Young men refuse employment. Fathers drop their kids off at school then rush home to play video games.

One may think this is an exaggeration but some of you are nodding your heads like *yup, I know guys like that.*

Another mark against video games is how it affects kids' moods. I've heard stories of boys becoming excessively violent when engaged with these games. Boys who grew up with sweet and respectful mannerisms develop rage seemingly out of nowhere. This is one of the hallmarks of addiction.

Finally, for the purposes of the discussion in this book, with so much time consumed with a controller in hand, children are not spending time with their families. I want a home environment where we are all interacting with each other on a regular basis. I don't want everyone in their own corner of the home, doing their own thing. We're not roommates. We are a family.

The benefit of entertainment does not balance the overwhelming negative effects of video games and for this reason, we've decided not to purchase video games for our home.

A Final Word

I wonder how many families are feeling disconnected. Living in the same house but no one is home. I wonder how many families are experiencing regular anxiety. How many families are discontent and not happy? How many families are well connected to the outside world but disconnected to those they snore with every night.

4.5 billion people actively used social media worldwide in 2021. 84% of Americans between the ages of 18 and 29 use social media. That's like all of them. Americans are spending just over 2 hours a day on social apps. When we're not thumbing through our phones, we're watching television. American families spent an average of 3 hours a day watching television in 2021.

Careers are taking more and more time and emotional currency from both moms and dads. Then we're choosing to give much of what remains to screentime. How much time and energy is left to connect with those who matter most?

My goal in this book was to first help your family stop the bleeding with 28 days to a healthier screentime culture.

Lead by apologizing for being the conduit by which such an unhealthy habit was allowed to fester. This is not a guilty apology, rather an acceptance of the role of commander-in-chief. The buck stops with you.

Let your family know that changes need to (and will) be made, but allow them time and space to process. Then take input from all stakeholders and decide on a plan to disconnect and reconnect to family.

At the conclusion of each week, check for progress and adjust. Tweak where necessary and celebrate the successes. Consider a more hands-on stance such as removing devices and helping your kids find alternative things to do.

Throughout the process, remain calm and resist the urge to blame and shame. This is not going to be an easy four weeks and your children should feel that you all are in this together as opposed to a feeling of punishment for a crime committed.

For parents who are starting out with young children, you have the advantage of being in a position to prevent the fire from starting in the first place. Decide if screentime will be a regular part of your child's routine.

How will you address boredom, eating out at restaurants, parent alone time, long rides in the car? Decide whether or not you will pacify with tablets and smartphones. But this must be a conscious decision, not a passive one.

If you believe, as I do, that children should spend time with each other, play with thinking brain toys and talk to other family members, then start thinking of all the amazing, creative things you will do as a family in lieu of screentime. I hope this excites you.

Talk with your spouse and draft a handwritten list of alternatives: nature walks, Legos, puzzles, reading, card and board games, cooking, house chores, gardening, and yes, being bored sometimes. Our job as parents is not to ensure our kids are never bored. Boredom is part of life and it's normal. We do, however, want to avoid chronic boredom.

This parenting thing is not a science. There are no laws of motion or formulas that spit out exactly one solution. There are multiple ways to skin this cat.

Each family will encounter their own set of challenges in trying to navigate a healthier screentime culture and those challenges will undoubtedly require unique solutions.

Some kids may experience different levels of withdrawal symptoms after a reduction in usage. Others may defiantly refuse to participate.

More often than in the past, children are sharing time between their mother's home and their father's home. Rules in the two homes may be inconsistent which may throw a wrench in the plan.

Frustration can come to a head at varying levels of the plan depending on personalities in the family and past experiences.

Every situation will be different and I want you to know that you will not follow a clear-cut path without having to stop at some point, and probably multiple points, and take a deeper look into this vital journey your family is taking.

I am here to help. At any time through this process, I am a quick email away and I will help pull you from the mud and get you back on the road. Please reach out to me at salehericali@gmail.com.

Amani-Rose Foundation
Donate at www.amanirose.org

E-mail
Send me an email (salehericali@gmail.com) with the subject "add me" to be added to the parent mailing list. You will be the first to know about new books, projects and events.

Instagram
@saleh.eric

Afterward
Asmaa Sallam

When I show up for work, I put on my neon yellow visibility vest, a hard hat and lace up my steel toe boots. When my husband arrives at work, all he needs is his heart. I work in a black and white, male dominated field, while Saleh works in a more artsy, emotional, female dominated profession. The careers we have chosen could not be more different and the manner by which we approach situations is reflective of this.

During our 12 years together, I've learned to approach things from a more ambiguous, whole-picture angle. This approach has been especially useful with parenting our children.

The idea of a drastic reduction in screentime usage is not popular. It goes against the culture. It goes against my instincts as a mother to entertain my babies with screens. Why not? It's available and convenient.

Because screens are not an every day option, our children are dependent on our time and attention. It would be nice to have more personal time for myself. I know it would be a lot simpler to give in and allow them access to ready-made entertainment. That would be the easy thing to do. But the easy thing is not always the right thing.

The results, I admit, are unlike a math equation. They are intangible and difficult to prove but I know they're there. We have been forced to lead by example and minimize our own screen usage. We cannot ask the kids to do something that we don't do. We are a happier family when we're not distracted. The four of us are more present and less annoyed.

We sleep better after a 20 minute walk in the neighborhood. Food tastes better when we eat together and talk. We don't feel like we're in survival mode and we have margin in our lives.

My message to parents who think this is an insurmountable obstacle is start small. It's not going to happen overnight. I promise you will feel a different vibe at home - a change that cannot be quantified.

Printed in Great Britain
by Amazon